"Astrology Theologised"

Valentin Weigel (1553-1588)

THE SPIRITUAL HERMENEUTICS
of
Astrology and Holy Writ

A TREATISE UPON THE INFLUENCE OF THE STARS ON MAN AND ON THE ART OF RULING THEM BY THE LAW OF GRACE:

Wherein is set forth, what Astrology, and the Light of Nature is. What influence the Stars naturally have on Man, and how the same may be diverted, and avoided.
As also
*That **the Outward Man**, how eminent soever in all Natural and Political Sciences, **is to be denied**, and **die in us**; and, that **the Inward Man by the Light of Grace**, through profession and practice of a holy life, **is to** be acknowledged and **live in us**: Which is the only means to keep the true Sabbath in inward Holiness, and free from outward Pollution.*
By
Valentine Weigelius.

SAPIENS DOMINABITUR ASTRIS

CHAPTER I.

What Astrology is, and what Theology; and how they have reference one to another.

THE Kingdom of Nature. — Astrology is Philosophy itself, or it is the whole light of Nature, from whence ariseth the universal natural Wisdom, or a solid, sincere, and exquisite knowledge of natural things: which light of Nature is twofold, external and internal: external in the Macrocosm, internal in the Microcosm. Or, Astrology is the very knowledge of good and evil, which is, and bears rule in Things subject to Nature; which Science flourishing in man, unless it be ruled and governed by Theology, that is Divine Wisdom, as the handmaid by her mistress, is vicious. And by her specious appearance and concupiscible jocundity, Man seduceth himself and, as it were by eating of the forbidden tree, or by whoring with the Creatures, he maketh his soul the Babylonian Harlot sitting upon the Beast, having seven heads and ten horns, and being sweetly deceived of himself, obtains eternal Death to himself.

THE Kingdom of Grace. — But Theology is the whole light of Grace happening to man from the Holy Spirit effused from above, which is the universal Wisdom of the Kingdom of Heaven, and the saving knowledge of divine and supernatural things, making chaste and purging the soul from every defilement of sin abiding in the mortal body in respect whereof that natural Wisdom is but a shadow, which, when the world is blotted out and removed, will together with it be blotted out and removed, and then Theology alone shall reign.

Astrology is so called because it ariseth from the stars; as Theology is so called because it flows from God. To live astrologically is, with a pleasing concupiscence, to eat of the Tree of the knowledge of good and evil, and to bring death to himself. To live theologically is to eat of the wood and Tree of Life by an intimate abnegation of oneself, and thence to attain to oneself, Life and Salvation.

The Light of Nature in Astrology, with its incitative fruits, is the probatory instrument whereby Man, placed in the midst, that is, between God and the Creature, is proved which way he would direct or convert his free will, desire, love and appetite; whether to God his Creator, by loving Him above all things, with his whole heart, with his whole mind, with his whole soul, and with his whole strength; which should be the Theological life. Or, whether, casting God behind, he would reflect to himself and to the Creature by love of himself, and arrogating of good things received, which was the Astrological Life at the Babylonish fornication, as will appear by that which followeth.

Astrology possesseth our soul with the eternal body, wherein the Light of Nature dwells and shines forth, in some more excellently, in others less. And it contains in itself two things.

1st. All kind of Sciences, Arts, Tongues, Faculties, and natural Studies: all the Gifts, as well of the mind, as of the body, and also all Negotiations, Occupations, Actions, and Labours of Men, how many soever of them are found, exercised and used in all times upon the whole Earth, everywhere amongst men, as well gross as subtle, as well old as new, serving as well to good as to bad uses.

2nd. Under Astrology, are referred all Orders, States, and Degrees of men, Distinctions of Persons, Dignities, Gifts, Offices, and every Kind of Life as well naturally ordained by God Himself, as thought of and invented by human wit, and found out in the whole world from the highest and most honourable to the lowest and most base.

All these are the fruits of the Stars, and have their original from Astrology, and pertain to the body and soul, and may be as well good as bad, according to the divers pleasures of the users and abusers.

But Theology possesseth our Spirit, which we have from God, which alone is *Theologus*, that is the Speech of God, the Breath of God, the Word of God, being and inhabiting in the Temple of our heart, from which alone according to sacred letters, true Theology is to be drawn forth; that is, the knowledge of God, of things divine and celestial and supernatural, arising from within, from the illumination of the holy Spirit Itself dwelling within us. According to Whose beck, will and command we ought to institute, direct and finish all our Sciences, Arts, Studies, Actions, Offices, Vocations, Industries, Labours and Kinds of Life, invented and drawn forth on Earth from the Light of Nature; so as whatsoever we think, say or do in the World, in all Arts, Sciences and Labours, it all proceeds from the Will of God, and seems, as it were, to be done and governed by God Himself in us, as by His fit instruments.

For every astrological gift, coming from the Light of Nature ought to be ruled and subjected. to the Divine Will by the Theological Spirit dwelling in us, that so the Will of the Lord be done, *as in Heaven, so also in earth*. For all Wisdom, both Natural and Supernatural, is from the Lord.

Astrology is the Science of Tilling and Perlustrating (PURIFYING or CLARIFYING) of the inferior terrestrial earth, ground, garden, Paradise, from which man was taken and made, as to his body and his soul, in the labour and culture whereof *six* days were ordained and appointed. But because this science of itself confers not salvation and eternal beatitude, but alone belongs to this present life; it is necessary the Lady and Mistress of all Sciences and Arts — Theology — be added, which seeing it is Wisdom from above, it hath in itself the science of tilling and perlustrating the celestial earth, ground, garden, Paradise, from whence also man was taken, created according to the similitude and image of God, which garden man also hath in himself, to the culture whereof, the *seventh* Day alone, which is the Sabbath day, is appointed.

For so it was ordained between God and man from all eternity, that Man should be God, and God, Man, neither without the other; that is, as God Himself is, and will be, the Paradise, garden, tabernacle, mansion, house, temple, and Jerusalem of man, so also was Man created for the same end, that he should be the Paradise, garden, tabernacle, mansion, house, temple, and Jerusalem of God; that by this mutual union and friendship of God with Man, and of Man with God, all the wisdom, power, virtue and glory eternally hidden in God should be opened and multiplied. For, God once made all things for Man, but Man for Himself.

CHAPTER II.

Concerning the Subject of Astrology.

THE study of Astrology or Philosophy is conversant about the universal knowledge of all the wonderful and secret things of God, infused and put into natural things from above in the first Creation.

The exercise therefore of the Light of Nature is the most sagacious perscrutation (INTENSE SCRUTINY) and enucleation (TO PEEL OUT or EXTRACT) of the abstruse, internal and invisible virtues, lying hid in external, corporal and visible things; to wit,

What should be the first matter of this great world whereof it was made.

What the Elements should be, and those things which are bred of the Elements, and consist in them; of what kind is their creation, essence, nature, propriety and operation as well within as without.

What might be in the stars of heaven, what their operation.

What in volatiles, what in fishes, metals, minerals, gems; what in every species of sprigs and vegetables.

What in animals, beasts, creeping things, and in the whole frame of the world.

Lastly, what is in Man, who was made and created of all these; to wit,

What is that mass, or slime, or dust whereof the body of the first man was formed, and whence he received his soul, and what it is; and whence he hath the Spirit, and what he is: And so the Light of Nature, or Astrology comprehends in itself all the wisdom and knowledge of the whole universe; that is, all these are hid and learned in the School of the Light of Nature, and are referred to as Astrology, or are rather Astrology itself; to wit,

The Subject of Astrology is therefore double; the Macrocosm and the Microcosm, the greater world and the lesser world.

The greater world is this very frame and great House, or this huge Tabernacle wherein we inhabit and live; and it consists of the four elements, Fire, Air, Water and Earth; and is twofold, visible according to the body, invisible according to the soul or spirit.

The lesser world is Man, the offspring or sum of the greater world, extracted and composed out of the whole greater world, who also in himself is twofold, visible according to the body, invisible according to the soul or spirit.

And as Man is made of nothing else but the world, so also is he placed and put nowhere else but within the world, to wit, that he might live, dwell, and walk therein, yet so as that he should take heed of that subtle Serpent, and should not eat of the Tree of the knowledge of good and evil, lest he die; that is, that he serve not the soul of the world, and creatures subject to vanity: but as a wise man rule the stars, and resist the devil tempting him, by the concupiscence of the flesh, of the eyes and pride of life; and suppress sinful nature, living and walking in wisdom and simplicity of the Divine Godhead inspired into him, not in the Subtlety of the Serpent by arrogancy and love of himself.

For it is most certain, of what anything is born and procreated, from thence also it seeks, desires and receives its nourishment, convenient to its essence and nature, for the sustentation of itself.

Now Man was taken from, and composed of the Macrocosm, and placed in the same: Therefore also necessarily he is nourished, cherished, receives his meat and drink, is clothed and sustained according to that. (Gen. iii, 19. Thou art taken from the earth, and thou shalt eat thereof in labour all the days of thy life, and shalt eat the herbs of the field until thou shalt return unto the earth, for from it thou art taken.)

Seeing therefore, Man, as to his body, is composed of the elements, and as to his soul, of the stars, and each part is fed and sustained from that from which it was taken; the food or aliment of the body, whereby the body grows to a due stature, comes to a man from the elements, the earth, the water, air and fire; not that man should take to himself for food the crude bodies of the elements, but the fruits growing from the elements: they are for nutriment. But the food of the soul inhabiting in the Microcosmical body, are all kinds of sciences, arts, faculties, and industries, with which she tincts and makes herself perfect.

Moreover; all aliment passeth into the substance of the user, and is made the same that he himself is; that is, whatsoever a man eats and drinks, the same thing is essentially transmitted into the substance, nature, propriety and form of man, by the digestion of *Archeus* in the ventricle (STOMACH). I say, the food passeth and is converted into the nature of the eater, and drink into the substance of the drinker, and is made one and the same with him.

And in the first place, let these things be understood concerning the body without wonder: because man is made of that which he eats and drinks. So also whatsoever a man learns, studies, knows in things that are placed without himself, that knowledge and intelligence passeth into the very essence, nature and propriety of a man, and is made one with him.

The Light of Nature is made man in man, and by a man's diligent searching, man is made light both in light and by light; and by the benefit of that light, he finds out all things, whatsoever he seeks and desires; but one more and another less, because all do not seek with the like study.

Every knowledge, science, art, industry and faculty passeth into the nature of man, penetrates him, occupies him, possesseth him, tincts him, is agglutinated to him, united with him, and perfected in him, and he in it. For, whatsoever kind of aliment man useth, and whatsoever he endeavours to study, inquire, know and understand, this is not strange or different from his essence and nature.

The reason is, because whatsoever is without a man, the same is also within him, for that man is made of all these Things which are without him, that is, of the whole universe of things.

Therefore whatsoever man takes from without from the elements and stars by meat, drink, knowledge, study and intelligence, this is the same that man is, and is made the same with man. So man eating bread, and drinking water, wine, etc., from the

Macrocosm, he eats and drinks himself; and learning — arts, tongues, faculties, and sciences of external things, he learns and knows himself.

And as he tincts his body by meat and drink, which pass into the substance of flesh and blood, so also his soul is tincted with whatsoever kind of sciences, arts, etc., eating and drinking, he is united essentially with that which he eats and drinks. And learning and knowing, he is united essentially with that which he studies, learns and knows. Wherefore this is a most certain rule; — *Whatsoever is without us, is also within us*. Which in this place, we, philosophizing of the soul and body, do thus declare.

This whole world visible as to the body, invisible as to its soul, is without us. From this we are all essentially in and with the first man complicitly made and created, and incontinently after the creation, were put and placed into it. And seeing it is manifest that everything that is derived, retains the essence, nature and propriety of its original; that although the Macrocosm is without us, yet nevertheless it may also be found truly within us; I say the World is in us, and we are in it, and yet this is, as that is without us, and we without that. For indeed we have no existence or original from anything else, but from that which is without us, and which was before us; nor are we, nor do we inhabit, walk and live in anything else, save in that whereof we are made. Neither do we seek and draw forth meat and drink from any other, either for the body or the soul, but from that into which we are placed, and which is placed in us.

As to the Spirit, we are of God, move in God, and live in God, and are nourished of God. Hence God is in us and we are in God; God hath put and placed Himself in us, and we are put and placed in God.

As to the Soul, we are from the Firmament and Stars, we move and live therein, and are nourished thereof. Hence the firmament with its astralic virtues and operations is in us, and we in it. The Firmament is put and placed in us, and we are put and placed in the Firmament.

As to the Body, we are of the elements, we move and live in them, and are nourished of them: — hence the elements are in us, and we in them. The elements, by the slime (SOFT, MOIST EARTH), are put and placed in us, and we are put and placed in them.

So God is whole without us, and also whole within us, by the being of inspiration, that is, by His Spirit communicated to us.

So the World is whole without Adam, and also the whole world is within Adam, by the being of extracted slime.

So Adam is whole without us, and also whole within us, by the being of seed.

And so we bear God within us, and God bears us in Himself. God hath us with Himself, and is nearer to us than we are to ourselves. We have God everywhere with us, whether me know it, or know it not.

We bear the world in us, and the world bears us in itself. Therefore whatsoever we perceive, feel, touch, taste, smell, hear, see, imagine, think, speculate, learn, understand, savour, know, eat, and drink, and wheresoever we walk, this is the very same from whence we have drawn our original. We are always conversant in those things of which we are made. For Man is the centre of the whole universe. So we learn nothing else, but the very same thing that was before us, and whereof we are made, and which before we begin to learn, lies hid in us. Yea, we learn, search and know nothing else than our *selves*; to wit, learning, searching and knowing that whereof we come, and whence we have received our being. So we eat and drink nothing else but ourselves, to wit eating and drinking that whereof we are made.

So our Body hath its hunger and thirst in itself from within, and desires the perfection of itself, by meat and drink taken from the elements from without.

See "Paracelsus" of the 'Lodestone of Nature in the Macrocosm and Microcosm'— So the soul hath its hunger and thirst in itself, and desires the perfection of itself, by meat and drink from the stars, which is the wisdom and knowledge of natural things; by arts, tongues, sciences, etc. Hence spring the artificers and wise men of this world.

Moreover, as in meat and drink taken from the elements, there is always pure and impure conjoined, which when they come into the stomach to the fire of digestion, are by the internal Vulcan or Archeus of Nature separated from one another after a spagirical (TO SEPARATE, THEN REASSEMBLE) manner, and that which is pure is retained and abides in us, that is the essence extracted from meat and drink, the pure is separated from the impure which passeth into flesh and blood. For it penetrates the body like unto leaven, and is made one with it, and causeth it to increase, that it may become greater and more solid in its strength and nerves; but the impure, differing from nutriment, is cast forth into the draught, and that by the operation of Archeus labouring in the ventricle. By like reason the matter is even in all sciences arising from the Light of Nature, where always good and evil are joined together. For in Nature all things are convertible, as well to good as to evil. Wherefore unless Astrology be Theologized, that is, unless that which is good be retained, and that which is evil rejected, Man from thence acquires to himself eternal death. And this is the probation of Man.

CHAPTER III.

Of the three parts of Man; Spirit, Soul and Body, from whence every one is taken, and how one is in the other.

THE parts of the Universe, of which the whole man is made, are three; — the World of Eternity, the Evial World, and the World of Time. The parts of man are three, Spirit, Soul and Body; and these three parts spring and are taken from these three parts of the whole Universe.

The Spirit of man comes from the Spirit of God, and participates with Eternity and *Ævo* (AEvo).

The Soul in man is extracted from the soul of the World, and participates with *Ævo* (AEvo) and Time.

The Body of Man is formed and composed from the body of the World, as elements, and participates with Time only.

The Body extracted from the elements, and constituted into this form, is the House, the Tabernacle, the seat of the Soul, and resident chiefly in the heart.

The Soul of Man extracted from the Soul of the world, and delivered over to the heart, is the habitation of the Divine Spirit, and hath the Divine Spirit in itself.

So one exists in the other, and dwells in the other, abides in the other, and operates in the other.

The Spirit in the Soul, and by the Soul.
The Soul in the Body, and by the Body.
The Body in and by external subjects.

Everything which is without is as that which is within, but the internal always excels the external in essence, virtue, and operation.

For *by how much any thing is more inward, by so much the more it is more noble, potent and capacious.*

Great virtue is in the Body, if it be excited.

Greater in the Soul of the firmament, if it be excited.

Greatest in the Divine Spirit, if it be excited.

By excitation all things are laid open, which are hidden and placed in Ignorance. For both Divine and Natural Wisdom sleep in us, and each light shines in darkness, and without excitation, man wants the having.

Great and excellent is the knowledge of the human body, extracted from the elements, and disposed into this form.

Greater and more excellent is the knowledge of the Soul, taken from the firmament, and inserted into the body.

Greatest and most excellent is the knowledge of the Spirit inspired from the Mouth of God into the first man, and by the mysteries of multiplication equally communicated to every one of us.

Wherefore is the knowledge of the human body great? By reason of its wonderful composition, that is, because all the four Elements are essentially composed in it. And moreover I say, the essence, nature, and propriety of all the Creatures of the whole *invisible* world which are in the earth, water, air and fire, are incorporated and situate in man. But seeing all things generally are conjoined and included into one skin, they are not altogether and at once discovered, nor can be revealed, but at least come forth and are known in *specie*, as they are drawn forth and excited.

Wherefore is the knowledge of the Soul which is in the heart of Man greater? Because the whole firmament, with all the essences, nature, virtue, propriety, inclination, operation and effect of all the Stars is therein conjoined and complicated, so as there is nothing in the whole power of the Spirit of the firmament or Soul of the World, which the soul of man also hath not in himself, and in the exaltation of itself, can give it of itself.

Yea, the whole Light of Nature is in the soul of the Microcosm, which is the wisdom and power and vigour of all things of the whole world throughout all the elements and things procreated of the elements. For she is the Astrological Spirit, containing in herself all kind of sciences, magic, Cabalistic, astronomic, with all their species, chemistry, medicine, Physic, all arts, tongues, all workmanships and all studies existent throughout the whole shop of Nature.

But because all these things are collected in one, and generally comprehended in the soul, they do not all lie open, or can they be in act together, although they are in power; but are let out and produced one species after another.

Wheresoever, therefore, these kinds of divers sciences flourish and are exercised amongst men, there shines the Light of Nature, and the soul of the Microcosm is in her exaltation, that is, the firmament of the Microcosm is in its ascendants.

But why is the knowledge of the Spirit of God greatest in us? Because He from Whom we receive this Spirit is greatest and most eminent above all. For in this same Spirit all the divine wisdom and power from whence that saving knowledge flows forth, that is, Theology, treating of supernatural, celestial and divine things, and is conversant in the Magnalia and mysteries of God placed above Nature, and tends even to the inexhausted and unspeakable profundity of the Deity, in which profundity, the very original matter, cause and end of all the works of God, and of things acted in time from the beginning of the creation even to the end of the consummation of the world, eternally and essentially lay hid. For all things came forth from Him; all things were made by Him, and all things consist in Him.

By how much anything is most inward, by so much it is more noble and excellent. This visible world is a body compacted of fire, air, water and earth, which is without, and hath in itself the spirit of Nature which is the soul of the world, which is within, to which soul this external body belongeth; because it is inhabited, possessed and governed by it. Hence the soul of the world is more noble than the body.

This soul of the world hath in it the Spirit of God, which comprehendeth and possesseth it. For nothing is beyond God or the Spirit of God. Hence the Spirit is more noble than the soul. *The more noble always exists in the more ignoble, and internals prevail over externals, as in essence as in power.* So our external body is indeed great in its stature and quantity, and a wonderful creature.

Yet the soul dwelling in the body is far greater, and more wonderful, not in corporeal quantity, but in essence, virtue and power.

But the Spirit is the greatest of all, not in the lump or corporeal quantity, but in essence, virtue and power; and therefore most wonderful.

There is nothing greater than that in which are all things. And there is nothing less than that which is in all smallest things Therefore let us observe this rule well:

By how much anything is more inward and more hidden from the external senses, by so much the more it is more worthy, noble and potent in its essence, nature and propriety.

Which we will demonstrate by examples. There is not any house built for itself, but for the inhabitant. Now the edifice is an external thing, and the inhabitant an internal thing. The house is for the guest, and not the guest for the house. Therefore the inhabitant is far more noble, worthy and excellent in his essence than every edifice, although sumptuous. For what is the house profitable, the guest being absent?

So garments are made and prepared for the body, that it might be and walk in them. Garments are external things; the body is internal. Therefore the body in its essence is far more noble and worthy than all garments, although precious. For, what need is there of garments, if they are wanting that which should put them on? Therefore garments are for the body, and not the body for garments.

So the body, raiment, house and habitation is a certain external thing to the soul, but the soul is internal.

And the body is for the soul, and not the soul for the body. Therefore the soul in her essence is a far more noble and worthy creature than the body, although most comely and most excellently proportioned. For, what availeth the body, the soul being wanting? It is but a carcase.

So the Soul, made and created for an habitation of the Divine Spirit, is external; but the Spirit is internal. And the soul is for the Spirit, and not the Spirit for the soul. Therefore the Spirit of God is found far more noble and excellent, and worthy in His original essence, virtue, nature, power and propriety.

So God is and abides the most inward, chief, great, potent, noble and worthy above all things; and contains all things in Himself, and He Himself is contained of none.

Everything that is most Inward is most precious and most noble. — Moreover, *by how much anything is more inward, by so much it is more nigh and near to us, but also so much the harder to be found and known.* Because of the too much aversion and alienation of our soul from divine and heavenly things; and by reason of the too much tenacity and adherency of our love to the creatures of the world.

And on the contrary; — *by how much anything is more exterior, by so much the more it is remote from us, and by so much the more strange.* For example sake; — the Spirit of the Lord truly is and inhabiteth in my soul, whose seat is in the captula of my heart: But, seeing every inhabitant is within, and its habitation without, it followeth; that the Spirit of the Lord is more near to me than I am to myself. And so it most evidently appears; —That the Kingdom of God is not to be sought without us, here or there, but within us;

— witness Christ himself who saith (Luke xvii), being asked of the Pharisees when the kingdom of God should come: *The kingdom of God shall not come with observation; neither shall they say, lo here, or lo there; for behold the kingdom of God is within you.* And the Apostle Paul (Rom. xiv), *The kingdom of God is not meat and drink, but righteousness and peace, and joy in the holy Spirit.* For by these he which doth service to Christ is accepted of God and approved by men.

The soul is and dwells in the heart, and the heart is in my body, therefore the soul is more near to me than the body.

My body is clothed with garments: hence the body is nearer to me than garments, and the soul nearer to me than the body: and the Spirit nearer than the soul: and therefore more noble, more worthy, and of more moment.

And because it is true, — that every internal is more noble and more worthy than his external, in which it is and dwells; that even all of us do witness, nilling or willing, knowing or not knowing. For behold, if we are in danger of life by fire, by water, by pestilence, or wars, etc., these being imminent upon us, then indeed in the first place, we leave behind us all our edifices, as well sumptuous as vile, with our external goods: and with a few things, if there be any we can carry with us, we betake ourselves to flight; so that the body being clad, might be preserved safe and unhurt, with the life and soul. By which very thing we testify, that the internals are more desirable than externals. For who would be so foolish that he would neglect, lose and destroy his body for the retaining of his edifices and external goods, when, the body being lost and destroyed, edifices and external goods are much more lost and destroyed. Furthermore, danger pressing, and necessity and straights urging us, and overwhelming us, with John the Disciple of Christ, we even leave and cast off our garments, with which we are covered, and whatsoever else is abounding to us of our substance, and naked and poor we commit ourselves to flight, that the body only with the life and soul may be preserved, and kept safe and sure. Do we not by this very thing point out and show that internals are better and greater than externals? — seeing that the body and life are internal, but vestments external. And who would be of so perverse a mind that he should embrace vestments with greater love than the body and life, and would in that mind persist in danger, that he would retain and keep his garments although he were compelled to lose and to destroy his body and life?

Moreover, in persecutions for the name of Christ, or for the truth, putting our body and life in danger, we even leave these and give them up to our enemies, to tyrants, etc., with patience, like the Lamb of God, whom all sheep imitate, only that the soul may be kept entire, strong, safe and uncorrupt, in the faith and knowledge of God and truth. Do we not signify by this, that internals prevail over externals? — because the soul is internal, the body external; and who would be of so foolish a mind, that he had rather neglect and lose his soul, with faith in God, and knowledge of the truth, only that he might keep his external mortal body, and temporal life? For faith and the knowledge of the truth being destroyed and lost, the body with the temporal life is of no moment.

Finally, in extreme torments, anguish and infernal dolours (DISTRESS) of our conscience for sins committed, even with David we leave and execrate (ABHOR) the very soul itself, and we bring to nought, and empty ourselves of all the solace both of God and the creatures, and we are left unto ourselves, crying out with the Son of God, "My God, my God, why hast thou forsaken me?" So that God only, and alone, might be, and remain in us, unhurt, unviolated, just and perfect in all things that He doth with us, both sweet and bitter. So, by adverse things, we are always reduced to internals, and make a regression to ourselves, and unto God which is in us. Do we not therefore after this manner testify the truth of this rule: — that every internal is more noble and more worthy than his exterior?

Wherefore, seeing there is nothing in us so near and intimate as God is, it follows that any other thing is not to be so esteemed, sought and loved as God alone, Who hath put and hid in us, the most excellent Treasure of His divine Wisdom, Light, Life, Truth, and Virtue, taken from His own Self, and hath commanded to ask Him, seek, and knock in the hidden place of our heart, in Spirit, and in Truth, having given a testimony, that the kingdom of God, first of all, to be sought, is not here or there without us, but is to be found most inward in us, as a Treasure hid in a Field.

From all these things it clearly appears to me that God is not at all more remote or nearer to me in this life whilst I am in this world, and in this mortal body, than He will to me be in life eternal. But I have and feel my God equally now present and intimate to me, even as I shall have Him in the other world, in a new body. For He is in me and I in Him, whether I am in a mortal body in this world, or without this body in that world. This alone makes the difference, that this thing even hitherto is hidden: but then it shall be manifest and open.

But that I am not so nigh and near to Him as He is to me, this is not to be imputed to Him, but to my aversion, who do not *sabbathize* in my God Who is with me, that is, who by running up and down with my unquiet and vagabond soul through the creatures, am more delighted to be and to be busied in my proper will out of my internal Country; and I suffer that ever hissing Serpent to creep on to the creatures in the multifarious concupiscence and delectation of the flesh, of the eyes, and pride of life, or self-love: neither am I less frequent in the various discourse of my thoughts, ever and anon, day and night, ascending out of my heart, now desiring this, now that, speculating, willing, nilling, now this, now that; where, moreover I weary and burden myself with all kind of care, and vex myself with various affections. All of which things are the Astrological operation and revolution of the internal stars in our soul.

But if I could Theologize my Astrology, that is, if I could desist sometimes from all these things, and study to be at rest in my God Who dwells with me, that is, if I could accustom my mind to quiet and spiritual tranquillity, that it should cease to wander in the variety of thoughts, cares, and affections, that it might be at leisure from the external things and creatures of this world, and chiefly from the love of myself; that I might wholly die, and as it were be annihilated in my self, that I could come into a loathing and oblivion, not alone of all the things of the whole world placed without me, and of mundane friendship, which I have with men, but also into a plenary dereliction of myself, that is, of my will, of mine — if there be any — wisdom, knowledge, science, art, industry, prudence; of mine — if there be any — dignity, praise, honour, authority, estimation in the world amongst men; of mine — if there be any — office, state, degree, order; and, in brief, into an absolute forgetfulness of all my negotiations and occupations, and of myself as well within as without, which is nothing else than to Theologize Astrology.

Then, at length should I begin: more and more to see and know the most present habitation of God in me, and so I should taste and eat of the Tree of Life, which is in the midst of Paradise, which Paradise *I myself am*, as a Guest with whom God is, and ought to be, and I in like manner with God.

This, I say, should be the exercise of my soul, the Theologization of Astrology, and a regression from Externals to Internals; from Nature to Grace; from the Creature to God; from the friendship of the world, to the friendship of God; from the tree of Death, to the Tree of Life; from terrene things to Celestial.

So should I go again to my first original, from whence I went forth, by arrogating to myself a liberty of willing, desiring, coveting, thinking, speaking and doing what pleased me, God in the meantime being neglected, without Whom I ought not to do any thing.

Whatsoever therefore we have from the Light of Nature, all this with most humble self-denial once in the week is to be laid down at the feet of the best and greatest God, whether it be magic, or cabalistic, or astronomic, or chemic, or medicinal, or physical science. Also liberal arts, and mechanic work, and whatsoever study, office, state, order, dignity, kind of life, also wealth, riches, houses, and all kind of natural gifts. All these appertain to this our Astrology, and ought so to be Theologised, by the exercise of sanctifying the Sabbath, which is an universal forgetfulness of all things and of ourselves, and the rest to our soul from all disquiet, in a sacred silence, a cessation from all will, thought, desire, affection, discourse, operation, etc., as well within as without. And this is that only and principle cause of the Sabbaths being divinely commanded to Man: —to wit, that man should not eat death and perish to himself by the eating of the forbidden Tree.

To eat is to be delighted in himself, and in the creatures, rather than in the Creator Himself. *Rom. I. I. Cor. 2. I. John 2. Matt. 6. Gen. 2. Exod. 20.*

To kiss himself in the gift received, neglecting the Giver.

To love the world, and things which are in the world, neglecting God.

To serve Mammon, neglecting God.

To use all things after his pleasure and will, despising the Law of the Lord. Thou shalt not covet, thou shalt not eat, thou shalt not desire to turn from God to the creatures; and to thyself; to commit whoredom with the creatures; to depend on thyself and on things created: to languish in love of terrene things, and temporal good things, setting God aside; which may be described a thousand ways.

Hence the Doctrine of Christ, who came from above, and brings celestial and divine wisdom from the Light of Grace, sounds altogether contrary, to wit: —

That a man ought to be converted into a child, and to have so much of the knowledge of good and evil to live in him, as he had when he was but a child, or infant newly born.

I say the Doctrine of Christ commands a man to eat of the Tree of Life, to live by the inspiration of the internal Godhead, which is, —

To fall off again from the creatures, and from himself to God.

To adhere to God, Mammon being left.

To be united with God, the love of the creatures being left.

To believe in God, to offer and give up himself to God, to pray - "Thy will be done."

To put off the old Man, and to put on the new Man.

To fly evil and adhere to good, which in like Sort may be explicated by a thousand manners of speaking and phrases from the very writings of the Apostles.

But in what manner all and singular kinds of sciences, and natural gifts, and those vain studies, actions, businesses and differences of men, etc., arise from the Light of Nature, or the Stars; and in what order they are referred to the Seven Governors of the world and how a man ought to use them; also how every one of us ought to Theologize his own Astrology flourishing in himself, and to erect to himself a new Nativity, from the heaven of the new

Creature, and to institute and assume a new kind of life; and chiefly, what is the solid and the most certain cause of all the holy Sabbath, that is, after what manner a man ought to labour six days and on the seventh day to sanctify the Sabbath rightly; — all these things are most evidently set forth and propounded in the following chapters of this book.

CHAPTER IV.

Of the composition of the Microcosm, that is Man, from the Macrocosm, the great World.

ADAM, the first parent of the whole human kind, was produced and formed by the admirable wisdom, and workmanship of God, as to his Soul and body of the slime or dust of the earth; which slime or dust was such a mass or matter, which had conjoined and composed in itself the universal essence, nature, virtue and propriety of the whole greater world, and of all things which were therein. I say that mass, slime or dust, was a mere quintessence, extracted from every part, from the whole frame of the whole world; from which slime or mass was made such a creature, with its form excepted, being one and the same with the great world, of which it was produced. Hence that creature was called Man, who afterwards, his admirable creation and formation being revealed amongst the wise, was wont most fitly to be called the Microcosm, that is, the little, or less world.

The absolute description, and essential explication of this slime, dust or mass, extracted from the whole macrocosm, we shall find everywhere abundantly and wonderfully declared, alone by *Theophrastus Paracelsus* in his most excellent writings.

Seeing therefore it is manifest, that every produced and composed thing can take or assume its essence, nature and propriety from nothing else but from that whereof it is made and produced; which even that first Man, *as another and later world*, made of the former world, by the *Ens* of that slime, is made partaker of the same essence, nature and propriety, as the Macrocosm had in itself. For the whole great world existing and being compact in that quintessence of extracted slime, forthwith it followed that the whole Macrocosm was complicitly collected and transposed into man, by divine formation, the substance and nature of the Macrocosm remaining nevertheless safe and entire. For such is the condition in the universal production and generation of things, that every like, of itself produceth his like, and that without destruction of its essence and nature.

John 3. That which is born of the Spirit is Spirit. That which is born of the flesh is flesh. — Hence that which hath its original and derivation from God, is the same that God is, — the Spirit or breath of God which is in man immediately proceeds from God: therefore God is of a truth in man by the *Ens* of inspiration.

That which hath its original and derivation from the world, is the same that the world is. The soul and body of man are immediately taken, extracted, and composed of the world, therefore the world is of a truth in man, by the *Ens* of slime.

So the first man, made of the Macrocosm, bears in himself the Macrocosm, with the essence and nature of all creatures complicated, collected, and compacted together: yet, nevertheless, he was formed as to his body of the elements and things elementated; as to his soul, of the soul of the Macrocosm, or the Spirit of Nature which contains and comprehends in himself the whole Firmament, with all its stars, and astralic virtues and operations. So it comes to pass that *there is nothing without a man in the whole heaven of Nature and in all the elements, with which Man in his composition doth not participate, and is endued with its nature.*

But there are two things in which the Microcosm and the Macrocosm differ, and appear to be contrary, to wit, — *the form of the person, and the complication of things.*

As to the form, it seemed good to divine wisdom, to convert that mass extracted from the Macrocosm, and to be converted into a man, not to put and set it into the form of the Macrocosm, which is round and circular; nor according to the animal form. But it pleased him to erect and apply it to the form of His own Image and similitude; man nevertheless, in the meantime, remaining the Microcosm.

Therefore, this difference does not touch his essence. The form doth not take away the truth of the subject, that man may not be believed to be the Microcosm. *See, concerning this, the 'Foundation of Wisdom' by Paracelsus.*

As to the complication or composition of all natural things into one body, or into one person, all things cannot be apparent and distinctly known together in a man; one Thing after another, as it is excited and provoked, is manifest and flourisheth in the species, other things in the meantime remaining hidden in the Macrocosm; all things are explicitly existing, living and operating in the species. But in the Microcosm all things are compact and conjoined together.

Moreover, after that Man, the Microcosm was, and held all things now in himself, out of which he was taken, behold the whole plenitude of Nature, as well corporally as spiritually, was conjoined in him, and as a most rich Treasure collected and laid up in one Centre, yet so as Man should be all Things complicitly; and yet none of them all explicitly.

Adam, Protoplastos. — And from this Protoplast, or first formed Man and begetter of all (Adam,) even in like manner are we constituted and formed: not of the same slime or mass as that was in the beginning, whereof Adam was made; but by a mass extracted from the substance of the Microcosm, which we, with Paracelsus, call the *Ens of seed*, which seed hath and bears in itself complicitly the whole Microcosm, that is, Man, and thence the human offspring, as to the essence, nature and propriety, in all things alike grows and comes forth to its begetter, as a most lively image, which truly could not be done if all these things did not lie hid and extant in the *Ens* of the seed. Hence every one of us hath the same in himself essentially delivered over to himself by the *Ens of the seed* from his parent, which the first Man received and had from the extracted Macrocosm by the *Ens of Slime*, to wit — an elemental body from the Elements, and a soul or Siderean Spirit from the Firmament.

CHAPTER V.

That all kinds of Sciences, Studies, Actions and Lives, flourishing amongst Men on the Earth and Sea do testify that all Astrology, that is, natural wisdom with all its species, is and is to be really found in every Man. And so all things, whatsoever men act on earth, are produced, moved, governed, and acted from the inward heaven. And what are the Stars which a wise man ought to rule.

IT is manifest therefore by the above-said, how man appeareth to be made at length as to his creation and formation of slime, that is, from the Macrocosm.

Because Man the Microcosm, placed in the Macrocosm, agreeth altogether as well with the whole Firmament, as with all the Elements, and is one and the same (his form only excepted) as we see redness to be altogether one and the same in wine and with wine, and whiteness in snow and with snow.

Then it followeth: — Seeing Man for himself and in himself is the whole world, as he which hath his proper Heaven, his proper Firmament, and Spirit of Nature, with the Sun, Moon, Planets, and all the Stars with him in himself, of which — *from within* — is constellated, inclined, directed, moves, excited, drawn, turned, governed, taught, illuminated, made joyful, made sad, is fortunate, and affected ; — it is manifest that he is in no wise forced and compelled by the *external* Firmament of the Macrocosm, or Soul of the World, that he should assume and take a mind and affections of willing, doing and operating this or that, from without, from the revolution and inclination, or constellation of the celestial stars in the Macrocosm.

For their opinion is of no moment, who, not rightly knowing the Macrocosm, are fallen into that error that they doubt not to determine that man, by the external influence of the stars, by a certain natural necessity is conditioned, predestinated, constellated, directed, compelled, and driven to this or that good or evil. Hence those false proverbs, — " the stars incline "— " the stars rule men," — which is in no sort so, if, according to their opinion, it be understood of the external Stars.

But we must know that all things whatsoever that are done by men, as well in soul as in body, arise and proceed *from within,* from their own proper inclination and nature.

Within, I say, in Man, is that Heaven, that Planet, that Sidus or Star, by which he is inclined, constituted, predestinated and signed to this or that ; and not from without, by the constitution of the external Heaven.

A wise man shall rule the stars. — And that saying— "A wise man shall rule the Stars," is not to be understood of the external stars, in the Heaven or Firmament of the great world, but of the internal stars, bearing sway and running, up and down in man himself; which will more and more appear by that which followeth. But this we premise for the beginning to be noted: —

That the external Heaven with its continual revolution, hath a most convenient correspondency with the inward Heaven in the Microcosm, and this with that; which you may thus understand : —

Whatsoever the figure of the external Heaven is, *in the point of conception of any man,* which happens in the matrix of the woman by the *Ens* of seed, even now sent forth from Man ; that man which is born and grows from that seed, receiveth from within, such a constitution of his nature, and life to be performed on earth.

Yet that constitution lies so long hid and unknown, that is, without act, in a naked power, until a man born into the world and educated to the use of free-will and reason, putting forth itself, begins to be moved and incited. For then, and not before, that constitution of his Heaven begins, by little and little, to roll, bring forth, move, and shew forth itself, when the Ascendants of that figure, by the imagination and fantasy, newly sprung up in the will and reason. arise and proceed to the motion of the mind and operation of the body. And so the internal Heaven in the Microcosm begins its motion and course, that a man, from within, from the guidance of his own Nature, begins to imagine, think, desire, hear, speak, do the same thing which before was signified, from the position of the external Heaven, *while he was conceived.*

Therefore the external Heaven in the Macrocosm, as it hath respect to Man, is, at least, a looking-glass and *perludium,* by which the Astrologer may look into, search, know, and describe what, and what kind of nature and propriety shall happen, and rule in him from the beginning of his nativity, to the end of his life — as he shall live Astrologically and not Theologically; — what, and what manner his imagination shall be, what his affections, what his cupidities, what his desires, what his manners, what his study, what his kind of life and death, with what he shall be adverse, and all things whatsoever seem to belong to the condition of human life. This, I say, may, from the position or erected figure of the external Heaven, be prognosticated and foretold ; not that those things are so done by necessity or coactive force, but only that those things are presignified, and, as it were, preludiated, and are, indeed, a certain picture of human life, as in like sort, a certain living man is painted by a painter, on the wall, from which picture his species and proportion, with all his habit, is exhibited and declared to be known. So also we men, living according to the course of nature, and not Theologizing our Astrology. are known, described and discovered, by an Astrologer from the Table-figure, face and concordance of the superior Firmament, as by a looking-glass.

For, living naturally, we have from the figure of Heaven, a natural description of our life, whether it be honest or dishonest, whether virtuous or vicious. Yet so as the impulsive or efficient cause of living thus may not be thought to proceed and be impressed on man from the external Heaven, but from within, from our internal Heaven, which is in our soul, delighted with this or that manner of living. For neither God nor the Macrocosm doth compel or force man, (placed in the midst,) from without, to this or that good or evil kind of life, by a certain natural necessity; but that very thing which is put into us by God, and by the Macrocosm, that is it whereby we are led, whereby we are constellated, moved, instigated, stirred up, invited, governed and inclined.

Rom. 6, *Galat.*5 — The one is the Spirit of God, the breath of God, the Deity and Heavenly Light, the holy Spirit, the Mind of God.

The other is the Spirit of Nature, the breath of the World, the Light of Nature, the affections of the flesh, terrene Wisdom, the animal man, the Siderean Spirit, the reason of Man.

Both lead to their Original, and shew what are theirs.

Our Nature instigates, moves, and leads to our naturals ; but the Spirit of God, which we have in us from God, instigates, moves, urges and leads us to supernaturals; that is, thither whence He Himself is.

There are, I say, two Inspirers, two Governors, two Captains, two Lords in us, to whom none of us can equally serve. The one tends to the straight way, to inherit and possess the Kingdom of Heaven, by contempt of the World, and denial of ourselves; the other, neglecting the Kingdom of God, to enter into the broad way. The one is of God, which is the Theological Spirit, propounding and persuading the Theological life to man; the other is from Nature, from the World, which is the Astrological Spirit, propounding, and persuading the Astrological life to man.

The Theological Spirit being endued with supernatural Light and Wisdom, shews the Kingdom of God, and eternal life.

But the Astrological Spirit, endowed with natural wisdom and light, shews the shop of Nature, and the glory of this world ; therefore those which are acted by the Spirit of God, these are the Sons of God, that is, who live Theologically. But they which are acted and led by the Spirit of Nature, (caring nothing, for the Kingdom of God, and the eternal country,) these are the sons of Nature, the sons of this world, animal men, not doing the will of God, but the will of the flesh: in which, with all their glory and magnificence, they, whosoever they are, how great soever they are, and wheresoever they are, must perish. For without the Theologization of Astrology, no mortal man can attain eternal salvation and beatitude. We must die once to flesh and blood, and to the whole animal man, and we must live to God; which life is altogether contrary to the worldly life. Of which more largely in the Epistles of Paul, and other Apostles.

But the stars, which a wise man is commanded to rule, are not those celestial stars extant in the Firmament of the Macrocosm, which are set before the Creatures of the Elements, that they might illuminate the earth, and be for signs and seasons, and rule over the day and the night; those have their peculiar Regent, Lord and Governor, to wit, the Spirit or Soul of the world, diffused into the seven Planets, and the rest of the Stars of the whole Zodiac, by which he exerciseth his rule and hath his influx into inferior things; therefore there is no cause that any should, through simplicity, think the dominion which a wise man hath over the stars, belongs to the moderation of the external Firmament; as if a wise man ought to rule the course of the celestial stars and signs, and to reduce the frame of the Macrocosm under his power; to direct and govern the Sun, Moon, Planets and Stars according to his pleasure; and to make calm and tempestuous weather according to his will. Not so; but the Stars over which we ought to rule, if we will be true wise men, are all the cogitations, speculations, cupidities, affections, etc., ascending, by imagination, out of our hearts, respecting the things and creatures of the world, and tending by free-will and reason to abuse and pleasure. To them we ought not to be too much addicted, or overmuch to connive and indulge. For in these, that deadly and infernal Snake or Serpent lieth hid, seducing man by all sorts of concupiscences into an unlawful love, honour and worship of the creatures, and thereof makes a Babylonish harlot; as in the subsequent matter will be demonstrated.

CHAPTER VI.

Touching a double Firmament and Star in every man; and that, by the benefit of Regeneration in the exercise of the Sabbath, a man may be transposed from a worse Nature into a better.

FROM the above-said, there appears a most elegant doctrine, to wit ; although some of us by constitution and concordance of the external and internal Heaven, in the point of his conception and nativity, should haply have attained the most wicked constellation and nature, ready and prone to commit any kind of maliciousness, so as he should even bear in his face, in his countenance, in his hands, and in his whole body, an evident signature or physiognomy to every most wicked crime, all which should shew most certain tokens that he should act only a most miserable and most wicked kind of life; but also should expect on himself the most cruel punishment and destruction. Yet, nevertheless, we must not altogether despair of such a man's correction and salvation. The reason is, because besides the natural Heaven, and Astralic Firmament which is in our soul, we have another Heaven, another Sidus, another star, another Light, another Constellation, which is the Spirit of God, by whose power being supported, we may shake off and drive away all the provocations of the evil ascendants of natural stars, as an ass is wont to shake off and drive away flies and gnats stinging him on his back.

Sibi Velit — Therefore although Nature is potent and strong in herself in inciting and forcing a man in his proper will and reason by her divers and delectable concupiscences to any kind of crime; yet the Spirit of the Lord in his virtue, power and fortitude, is far superior, and exceeds Nature in as great a measure as the Sun is seen to excel the Moon. Let a man then at length learn, and do his endeavor that he may know what that most profitable precept of God, touching the sanctification of the Sabbath to be exercised every seventh day requires of him, in which exercise, nevertheless, the worst of things may be corrected, and also transformed into the best things. For such a medicine lieth hid in the holy exercise of the Sabbath, as whole Nature, with her universal virtue is not able to exhibit to a man; for which medicine's sake, this book is written.

A man, therefore, inclined naturally to this or that vice, by occasion of his generation, ought not to connive at himself, or to frame any excuse, as if he could by right accuse the external heaven that it is the cause, wherefore he cannot live honestly and do that which is good, nor by any means can overcome, chance, break, correct his sinful nature, or convert it into better; and so under the pretext of human imbecility, as it were, defend his spontaneous malice, avarice, lust, pride and intemperance, etc., and to go forward in a vicious life.

O opinion most worthy of refutation, and to be accursed! I pray, what should the cry of Christ, the Prophets and Apostles avail? Repent, repent, be ye converted unto me, and I will be converted unto you; put off the old man, and put on the new man; and fly evil, and cleave to that which is good; and lay aside the works of darkness, and walk in the light! I say, to what end should these things be spoken and commanded, if our defence or excuse should have place in the divine Judgment?

Let such a man, therefore, so wickedly deceived of himself, suffer himself to be instructed and taught by this our most profitable Theologization of Astrology, wherein we have found and tried, not without the greatest joy of the mind, that besides the shop and operation of Nature, there is always present in us something far more great and excellent, with the knowledge and virtue whereof we being fraught, have power of resisting not only one, but all vices, as well the greatest as the least, whatsoever lie hid and are manifest in us. Yea, power not only of casting down, and drowning one stone, but also the whole mountain of the Microcosm being in us, in the Sea of divine Power; or extirpating utterly, not only one leaf, but even the whole tree of the knowledge of good and evil extant in us, and of transplanting it into the garden of the celestial Paradise.

Mark this. — For so all these things are manifest in Theological Mysteries to those that understand these things. *Truly, it is evident, all things are Essentially to be transferred unto Man, which are divinely written for Man.*

See the Scripture, of Regeneration and New Birth. — I say, we have a power lying hid in us of over-ruling whole Nature, of stopping the Serpent, and overcoming all his force, and of instituting in us a new, and that a good — a better — the best Nativity ; of erecting and instituting in us, from a new Heaven, a new kind of Life, and a far more happy figure, and that by the sole benefit of the Sabbath; by which, from day to day we may put off the old man, and put on the new man; fall back from vices, and pass on to virtues, that is, to shake off from us all the ascendant stars or flames of divers concupiscences and desires to all kind of pleasures of this world, ever and anon provoking, drawing, and seducing, us.

John 17. — By this means we go forth safe and free from the House of Egypt; from the Babylonian Captivity ; and we escape from the power of the great Creature ; we overcome sinful Nature, we resist the Serpent, we chase away the Devil. And by how much the more frequent we are in this exercise of the Sabbath, or in this Theologization of Astrology, by so much the more are we made strangers to Nature, that we are scarce any more known or touched by her, neither doth any Astrologer, Physiognomist, Signator, Divinator, artist how industrious soever, know any more to erect any certain nativity, or to prognosticate any thing, to come. Because they which are frequent in familiarity with God, these are more and more alienated from the world, that they are not any more said to be of the world, but of heaven, although as to the body, they are as yet conversant in the world. And whatsoever any one doth by the Sabbath, in the introversion of his mind, he acts and orders with God, and God with him, in the hidden place of his heart; this cannot be seen or known by any spirit, much less by man.

Rom 12. — In brief, by the Sabbath alone, the Phoenix of our Soul is renewed, who, altogether denying, deposing, refusing and accompting for nothing all the vanity of this world, and itself from within and without, plainly dies in the forgetfulness and contempt of all things, and of itself, and offers itself a living and pleasing sacrifice to God and, being regenerate anew, becomes a new creature, a new offspring from the seed of the Woman, by conception from the holy Spirit, is made a Son of God, a new man, an imitator of Christ, following his steps; is made a hater of evil, and a follower of good ; a new plant, a new tree that is good, which brings forth good fruits. This is true repentance, true penitence, the true putting off the old man.

Here some Astrologers are to be admonished of their want of knowledge, who have not doubted to subject even the whole man, with all things which are in him, to the dominion of the world and stars, in erecting their nativities as if a man were or had no more in himself than a brute or beast, through ignorance passing by the constitution of Man in three parts — Spirit, Soul, and Body; whose soul arising from the firmamental zodiac, and whose body from the elements, are altogether subject to the dominion of Nature. But not the Spirit, which we have from God; and listening, nothing, to that, which every disciple of Christ and friend of God, regenerate from above, by faith and the death of sin in the most holy Sabbath, hath within himself, a most present medicine in his heart, against all the poisonous and deadly wounds of nature, and the Serpent; and also the divine commandment of deposing, overcoming, and conquering, the old heaven, with its inclinations of divers concupiscences, and of walking in the newness of the Spirit, in the Light of Grace.

The exercise of the Sabbath, or Theologization of Astrology, is to die to thyself and the whole creature; to offer thyself wholly to God, with all things which are within and without. Hither belong all the Scriptures, and all books speaking of the mortification of Man. — To wise men, therefore, that is, to those that know both God and themselves rightly, the matter is far better to be looked into, for they know both are in us: —

God, and Nature.

The Kingdom of Heaven, and the Kingdom of the world.

The Tree of Life, and the Tree of Death.

The greater Light, and the lesser Light.

The seed of the Woman, and the seed of the Serpent.

And also that Man is placed between these two, to be exercised in this world in a perpetual war, whether of these should overcome ; thence shall man have his reward, for God will render to every one — all crafty excuse and imbecility being laid aside — according to his works, whether they be good or evil.

Here you shall observe an example, touching the change of man from an inferior and worse nature into a superior and better nature. If you take a certain stone, lying, by chance in a sunny place, and very much heated by the too much parching heat of the sun, and put it into water or some river, then the sun can no more make it so hot, or penetrate it with his heat; in like manner the case is in the Theologization of Astrology. Take or gather, and apprehend all thy evil nature, and thy insincere affections, and unlawful lusts, too much operating and flourishing in thee; I say, take and put them by the Sabbath, into the mind, or spirit of thy mind, which thou hast from God, who is the everlasting fountain and water of life; and sabbathize in a solid and constant abnegation of thyself, and of all things known unto thee, which are within thee, as well as without thee, that thou mayest almost wholly die there; then will thy soul with all her adherent stores of concupiscences, fall down and be drowned in the depth of the supernal water, which is the Spirit of God infused in us; and the firmamental operation will more and more cease and be wearied in thee, and the ascendant stars of thy concupiscences will no more afflict, urge, drive, carry thee as before ; but, from day to day, thou shalt ease thyself from that most hard yoke of the Zodiac, and of all the Planets; thy youth shall be renewed as an Eagle. and thou shalt be like an infant new-born, and shalt perceive in thyself new virtues, and affections to work and move in thee, arising, inclining, occupying, leading and governing thee from the celestial Star, and influence of the divine Spirit. So as where, heretofore, thou hast been the servant of sin, and hast given thy members weapons of unrighteousness and malice, now with trembling thou abhorrest the performances of thy fore-past life, and fraught with a new mind, heart, affections and desire, from the exercise of the Sabbath, by the Spirit of God, hereafter thou shalt serve God, and give up thy members weapons of justice, piety, charity, mercy, meekness, temperance, modesty, chastity, and so thou shalt rightly Theologize thy Astrology, so shalt thou best overcome, correct, amend thy nature, so shalt thou rightly tread the head of the Serpent under thy feet, so shalt thou well silence in thyself the assaults of the devil.

Hence the true Sabbath instituted and commanded of God, is the best cure and medicine against all kind of evil, — which quickly brings death eternal to the soul, and temporal to the body, by which we may put off, bear and take off that great and most grievous yoke and mountain of so great a Zodiac, of so great a Firmament, of so great Governors. I say, to take away the Kingdom of Rule, and to precipitate into the immense Sea of eternal water, and ever and anon get new strength, and come out more vivacious, as was well known and used by the Patriarchs in the first age, whence also they could yet to themselves the Enochian long life upon earth, by the exercise of this kind of mental Sabbath, which, indeed, is altogether obliterated, abrogated in this our age, and seems to be a thing unknown.

But how every one of us ought, and may know, and try in himself, what and what kind truly is his Astrology or firmamental action or operation of the Light of Nature; and how he may and can Theologize the same, that is, overcome Nature and be made the Son of God, this the following Chapters will illustrate, and teach more clearly than the Sun.

CHAPTER VII.

Touching the Distribution of all Astrology into the Seven Governors of the World, and their Operations and Offices, as well in the Macrocosm as in the Microcosm.

THE whole shop of Nature, with all her sorts of sciences and actions, is ordained and distributed into Seven chief members, Kingdoms or Dominions according to the Seven Astras of the Planets; of the Sun, of the Moon, of Mercury, of Venus, of Mars, of Jupiter, of Saturn. who are the Governors of all natural things extant in the whole frame of the World by the four Elements.

But the Light of Nature, which we call Astrology, is nothing else than the very life, vigour, virtue, action and operation of the whole world, in things, which proceed and come forth from the Soul of the World, or the Spirit of the Firmament; whose seat is in the body of the Sun. For there the Soul of the World, or the Spirit of the Macrocosm dwells, as the Soul of the Microcosm in the heart, and in the sun it is most potent, whence it diffuseth his virtues, actions and powers, out of itself ever and anon into the other six Planets,— the Moon, Mercury, Venus, Mars, Jupiter and Saturn. And, moreover, in all the other Stars, being throughout the whole stelliferous chaos.

By this only Soul the whole World lives, is governed, agitated and moved, as a body by its spirit.

The Sun is the heart and light of the World. In this heart, I say the Soul inhabits, which illuminates all and every the Planets and Stars upwards above itself, and downwards beneath itself, as well in the day as in the night time, and disperses its power into all and singular bodies, as well the superior things to the utmost superficies of the frame, as also the inferior things even to the inward centre in the earth.

Yea, the Sun by his virtue passeth through all corporeals like unto glass, and operates in them without any impediment.

The power and working of the Sun. — So his force penetrates the whole body of the sea as glass, without any obstacle, even to the lowest bottom thereof; so the whole body of the earth, full of pores on every side, is passable to the Sun, even to the inward point of its Circle. So the Sun fills the sphere of Air; also the spheres of Heaven, and enters into views, and possesseth with his power all the Angels of all the regions and parts of the World, as the Soul doth the body of the Microcosm; and not only the Chaos and the bodies of Elements, but also all the generations and substances of all things whencesoever existing, as well subtle as gross, as well light as heavy, as well soft as hard; metals, mountains, hills, gems, rocks, stones, wood, and whatsoever is, everywhere, so as it reacheth to the very centre of the earth; neither is his force and operation wanting, or deficient there. For all bodies though never so great, gross, thick, are altogether as glass to the penetrative power of the Sun, and although our eyes do not so expressly know and see this present ingressive, penetrating, subtle and active power of the Sun in all things, but the gross bodies always are and remain in our eyes gross, dark and shady, yet in respect of the Sun, and to the virtue of the Sun, after their manner, all things are diaphanous and perspicuous, and penetrable. Which solar virtue thrusts forth and produces all things hid in the earth: and, also, the air is such, that with the very virtue of the Sun, it doth essentially enter into all bodies, penetrate and fill all things. *Life is Fire.* — For fire is the life of things; no fire can burn, that is, live without air, wheresoever therefore there is life, or fire, or the virtue of the Sun, there also is air. *The World a great Creature* — Now the whole greater World, as to its soul and body, with all the creatures that are therein, is one Creature by itself, and one animal, and lives like an animal, having in itself its vital Spirit, endued with a Sevenfold operation, or diffused into the seven Planets, into all the Stars, and into all the elements, and all vegetables, minerals and animals generated of elements. The element of Fire hath his shop or seat in the body of the Sun, Planets and all the Stars; in that fire the Phoenix of the world, or Soul of the world, dwells, which operates all things, and is the Light of Nature, the Vulcan of Heaven, the Archeus of Nature.

The Air is its respiration and balsam, the Water is its blood, the Earth is its flesh. In like manner also it is in the Minor World, or Man, who, as to his soul and body (the form excepted) in all things answers to the Major World, as a son to his father, because taken out of him, and placed in him.

In the heart, is the seat or habitation of the soul of the little world, or the Siderian Spirit, whose virtue, life, motion, nature, force, operation, ever and anon by going forth, diffuseth itself into the other six principal members of the Microcosm, — the Brain, the Liver, the Lungs, the Gall, the Spleen, the Reins, and from thence into the whole body, and all the muscles, veins, nerves, parts and extremities of the whole Microcosm ; and so, that only Soul, resident in the Heart, carries, governs, agitates, leads, moves the whole body, according to the nature and propriety of these Seven principal members; by which the body performs all his works, as well artificial and subtle, as simple and rude.

As the soul of the Macrocosm, labouring in the Seven Governors of his body, and the rest of the stars, produceth all created things.

Therefore, as to the concordance of these seven Governors, Planets, Stars, or Virtues in the Major and Minor Worlds, it is certain that

1. The Heart	In the Microcosm is the same, and hath the same force, as hath	1. The Sun ☉	In the Macrocosm.
2. The Brain		2. The Moon ☽	
3. The Lungs		3. Mercury ☿	
4. The Reins		4. Venus ♀	
5. The Gall		5. Mars ♂	
6. The Liver		6. Jupiter ♃	
7. The Spleen		7. Saturn ♄	

And as to the Elements,

1. The Flesh	Hath each its anatomy of the Microcosm	1. Earth	Of the Macrocosm.
2. The Blood		2. Water	
3. The Respiration		3. Air	
4. The Heat		4. Fire	

For in the Flesh of the Microcosm lieth hid the essence, nature and propriety of all vegetables springing out of the Earth, compacted and dispersed throughout the whole body.

In the Blood doth exist the essence, nature and propriety of all minerals and metals bred of Water, dispersed throughout the whole region of the blood.

In the Respiration, whose seat is in the Lungs, the Bowels, and the Veins, and all pores, muscles, etc., is the essence, nature and propriety of all the airy creatures, dispersed through the whole body.

In the Heat dwells the essence, nature, force, operation, and propriety of all the Stars, and constellations of stars, dispersed through the whole body.

Moreover, as to the concordance of either Light, as well in the Major as in the Minor World, thus it is.

Also, the fruit of the Tree of knowledge of good and evil, which is evident only to Magians. —Whatsoever things man living on earth hath found out, first theoretically, by speculating, meditating, searching and inquiring,, excogitating, from within in his heart and after by his free Will or desire produceth, endeavours, attempts, institutes, handles, operates and transfers to practice in whatsoever kind of Sciences, Arts, Faculties, (Theology excepted, which is not a human invention) studies, handy works, labours and negotiations, whether they be referred to good or evil, —all these comprehended under one name, are called the *Light of Nature, or* Astrology, or Natural Wisdom, arising from the Natural Heaven, or Firmament and Stars. That wisdom and that light are in the Soul of Man, dwelling and working in the heart, which, if it be exalted in its power given to it, and created in it, can do the same, and more, than the soul of Nature in the Macrocosm, whose seat is in the Sun; because Man the Microcosm is the quintessence, extracted from the Macrocosm.

But, seeing all and singular Sciences, Arts, Faculties, Orders, States, kinds of Life and Studies flourishing amongst men on the earth, arise and proceed from an internal invisible Heaven, Firmament, Star and Light of Nature, in the Microcosm, which is extracted from the Light, Heaven, Firmament, and Star of the Macrocosm, and hath its singular anatomy, distribution and conveniency to the offices and operations of the Seven Governors of the World without, we, as the order of those Governors extant in the Firmament of Heaven is exposed to our eyes, will first of all handle *Saturn*, occupying the supreme sphere; to wit, what is the theory and practice of his Heaven, Star, or constellation, with his adjunct stars in the Macrocosm; that is, what is his condition, nature, propriety, virtue and inclination, what Science, what Art, and Industry, what Order, what Study, what Fortune, what good and what evil men draw and handle from him on the earth.

Whereby it will appear that Saturn is not only without a man in the Major World, but also in man, with all the legion and inclination of the adjunct stars.

Then, how the whole Astrology, —that is, the nature, propriety and operation of this Planet—ought to be Theologized, by the exercise of the Sabbath.

CHAPTER VIII.

Touching the Astrology of Saturn, of what kind it is, and how it ought to be Theologized.

SATURN, as to the description of his substance and nature in the Macrocosm, is one of the chief of those seven stars, which we call Planets, or Governors of the World walking next of all in the aerial region under the Firmament or Zodiac, and ordained in a certain Sphere or Circle, or Mansion; the circuit of circle he finisheth he passeth over once in the space of thirty years time, through the twelve celestial signs extent in the Zodiac. His body arising from the element of Fire, and illuminating, that is cherishing, and governing the earth, and what are in and on the earth, — his body is fiery and globulous, his astralic force, which is the firmamental or Siderian Spirit, is invisible.

Now Saturn is conditioned with that nature and propriety from the first creation, that he may send forth and exercise the virtue and operation of his splendor and light in his subjects existing here and there in the four elements, as are vegetables, minerals, animals, properly, and in species, pertaining to him, wherein he effects and frames such a nature and virtue, as he hath in himself. Now Saturn hath his subjects appropriate to himself in every kind of creature; amongst vegetables he hath his young twigs, his herbs, his plants, his flowers, his trees, on which he operates by his influence after his manner. So amongst minerals and metals, also amongst animals, creeping, going, cattle, beasts, watery and volatile creatures.

For the whole university of the creatures of this world, with us men, is divided into seven kinds or assemblies, and dispersed into every region, which answer to these seven Governors, in their natural virtues and proprieties, as well internal as external.

But, touching the Astronomical condition of Saturn, and the rest of the Planets, to wit, what kind of motion, position, course, quantity, distance, opposition, conjunction, and other dimensions of this kind they have amongst themselves; also touching, the difference of their weights in metals, etc., it is not our purpose here to handle them; concerning such kind of things, consult Astronomical books, and Chemical books and the like, publicly extant abroad; but we rather handle and shew this :—How all the studies and offices and kinds of life of all men have their original from the stars, and to which Planet every thing is to be referred. Then, how the whole Astrology ought to be Theologized, that is, how every one of us ought to know, discern, hate, put off, lay aside, and deny the old man made of Astrology, with all his Wisdom, science, knowledge, prudence, industry, art, and whatsoever a man hath, occupies and possesses of the gifts of Nature; and in the denial of himself and all that he hath, as well within as without, altogether to grow a child again, to be made an infant, yea a fool; and to put on the new Man, which is created according to God, to walk in newness of life, to die to sin, and to live to justice; to know that Babylonian harlot and her Beast, and to preserve himself from her; to know the forbidden

Tree, and to eat of the Tree of Life, and to pass over from nature into grace, to be made a new creature, to be born again, to transplant himself from the terrene Paradise into the Heavenly; to labour six days, and rightly to sanctify the seventh, and the like. This is the intention, end and scope of this our work.

Therefore, Saturnists, or the worshippers of Saturn, whose minds, desires, wills, inclinations, affections, concupiscences, pleasures, cogitations, speculations, inventions, actions, and labours are ascribed to Saturn, as to their study, and kind of life, are men in whom is and flourisheth all kind of science and industry.

1.*Cain was a husbandman; Abel a keeper of sheep.* — Of all Agriculture; as are husbandmen, countrymen, farmers, tillers of the ground; also mowers, threshers, herdsmen, swineherds, pastors of cattle, purveyors of corn, or those who exercise merchandise, with corn and pulse; also dressers of vineyards, that purge wines, gardeners, and briefly, all agriculture, with all its species.

2. *Jubal was the father of inhabitants in tents, and feeders of sheep. Tubal Cain found out every artifice of brass and iron.* — The whole art and science, edificatory, as under; with all kind of artificers, and workmen, comprehended, as rough masons, stone-cutters, carpenters, joiners, and in brief, the whole administration of *economy,* or household affairs, joined with parsimony and frugality.

3. The whole art and metallic science, which teacheth the manner of searching and trying the bowels of the earth, and of digging minerals, metals and riches, the provocations of evils; also *Treasurers,*

and whosoever seem to seek and take their livelihood from the earth by the the labours of their hands, as are potters, tile-makers, bearers of dead bodies, fishmongers, root-sellers, colliers, and others of this kind ; and also clothiers, linen-weavers, shoemakers, cobblers, cardmakers, etc. Also solitary men, as monks, hermits, and like to these.

As touching the mind, and vices, Saturnists are avaricious men, covetous of gain, usurers, lenders for gain, Jews, toll-gatherers or publicans, tenacious, livers sparingly, Mammonists, altogether watching for their proper commodities. Also thieves, robbers, makers of false money, sergeants, false judges, hangmen, enchanters, evildoers ; also men austere by nature, froward, more sad than joyful, thoughtful, melancholic, fantastic, very silent, tedious, infidels, sacrilegious, and what kinds of life soever of this sort.

Likewise, *philoponoi,* laborious, full of business, tumbling, macerating and wearing themselves in continual cares, and furthermore in whatsoever appears like to these.

As to the quality of the body, and external manners, Saturnists are men worn with years and age as well men as women, covered with gray hairs, with a slender and lean body, thin beard, eyes lying deep in the head, with a neglected form, and not amiable, always looking grimly *agelasoi,* halting, beggars, often sick, etc.

All these studies, and all and singular kinds of life of men, as they are formed and seen abroad amongst all nations, people, kindreds, etc., of the whole compass of the earth, are referred to the heaven, region, dominion, nature and inclination of Saturn.

I say, all these kinds of men, with all their studies and kinds of life, as well honest as dishonest, as well good as bad, as well private as public, are worshippers of Saturn, for that in the handling of Saturn, that is, in the drawing forth of the nature of the Saturnine light, they spend their labour and time; and by diligent study and inquisition they draw forth, search, produce and manifest those things of Saturn which are in natural things.

All the industries, inventions, arts, actions and labours of these men in every season, have proceeded and as yet do proceed, *from the internal invisible heaven,* which is in the Microcosm ; and are part of the Light of Nature, in which man walketh, whether well or ill, honestly or filthily, according to the diversity of his flexible will and desire, as well to good as to evil ; and men are busied about the external subjects of the Macrocosm, without which, vain were the vigour and endeavour of the Light of Nature in man. For every action of the Microcosm from within, tends to the subjects of the Macrocosm without; because there the works of man are perfected or performed. For indeed man hath from the Light of Nature in himself, the science of ploughing and tilling the earth, and fields, building houses, of seeking and handling metals, etc., but he hath not in himself the subjects, matter and instruments ; therefore he takes them from the Macrocosm, and perfects his work, found out and excogitated by the Light of Nature. Thus, seeing all the external works of men arise from within, from the invisible revolution of the internal stars, ever and anon ascending and shining forth by cogitations and imaginations, and are perfected by external operations and labours, we may from every work of man, see and know the constitution of the internal heaven, what kind of position, what ascendants, what motions, constellations and inclinations every artificer hath; where it is wonderful to behold the variety of the Natural Light. Hence, by how much the more the artificer doth appear in external works, by so much the more and more perfect, hath the constitution and influence of the internal heaven, been with the workman.

Therefore we must know that every species, of whatsoever science, art and faculty, is a singular constellation, star, inclination and influence, ascending from the inward heaven, and shining, acting and operating one by one in man ; therefore all the cogitations, imaginations, inventions, desires, studies and intentions of Saturnists bent or inclined to good or evil, are the Astras or stars ascending from the inward heaven, and are the operation of the Saturn, of the Microcosm, in the soul, with his stars agreeable to himself, in which cogitations and operations that crafty Serpent, which almost none in this our age seems to know, is powerful and rageth, by leave permitted to him by God, to tempt and prove man, (placed in the midst,) by these delights of the Light of Nature, and of the things of this world, and to bend the will, love, desire, and concupiscence thereof from good to evil, from God to the creature, whereunto man, (O grievous!) is too ready and prompt.

Truly innumerable and infinite are the multitudes of men living on the earth which are found in this kind or practice of Astrology. For it is, (which we would have mystically spoken) one of those seven congregations or generations of the World, or people worshipping the Queen of Heaven, or venerating, and worshipping the Babylonian harlot, and adoring the Beast endowed with seven heads and ten horns. And this is the sense which sleeps with wisdom, which will appear better by the following things.

Now, as the external heaven in the Macrocosm, always and ever and anon is rolled and turned about with a perpetual motion; and always other and other stars are seen to appear ascending and always descending, so as there is a perpetual mutation and vicissitude of the actions of Nature, labouring in the greater World, where now it is winter, now spring, now summer, now autumn, now day, now night, now fair weather, now tempest, now snow, now rain, now winds, now storms, now this, now that, etc., which are all the Astralic operations of the heaven of the Macrocosm : —so also in like sort is the course, vicissitude, motion and revolution of the stars, ever and anon ascending. and descending in the heaven or Soul of the lesser world ; that is, the soul, or our siderean Spirit, is an unjust spirit, wherein the ascendant cogitations, new concupiscences, various desires, are always moved, excited and felt, now willing this, now willing that, now so, now thus, now we rejoice, now we sorrow, now we are beaten and agitated with these, and now those affections, now we are occupied with these, now with those businesses and labours, all which are nothing else than the Astrology of the Microcosm, to be Theologized in all of us that are willing to use them piously.

But how and wherefore ought the Astrology of Saturn to be Theologized in Man ? If thou askest me, wherefore and how all the natural sciences appertaining to the Astrology of Saturn, together with all the kinds of the Saturnine life, ought to be and may be Theologized, I again ask thee, that thou tell me the cause wherefore, according to that great precept of God, we ought to labour and finish our work in six days, but the Seventh day to sanctify the Sabbath ? Or wherefore we cannot enter into the Kingdom of God, and possess beatitude in eternal life unless we shall be converted and be made as infants ? For these have one and the same reason and cause, tend to one, will one, and belong to one.

The answer therefore is ; — Therefore we ought to Theologize Astrology, therefore we ought to labour six days and sanctify the seventh, therefore we ought to be converted and become as infants, because nothing at all but the New Creature, the new Man from Heaven, he that is regenerate from above, he that is born again of immortal seed, is required to the possession or acquisition of the Kingdom of Heaven. Not the old man from the earth, seeking earthly things, gaping after earthly things, rejoicing in earthly things, occupied and delighted in earthly things, loving, possessing, favouring earthly things. I say, not such, but as we have now said, the man born again from above, seeking those things which are above, and not those things which are below, not arising from the will of the flesh; and not of the will of man, but of God.

But to the end that we may be the better understood of the ruder sort, first we will handle a few things in general.

What is the Theologization of Astrology?

Afterwards we will set upon our Saturn, with his professions and faculties, where we shall demonstrate to the eye, that in the sole Theologization of Astrology is to be sought and found the gate of Paradise, to eat of the Tree or wood of life, which is in the midst of Paradise, etc. Also, what is that strait gate that leads to life, which few find ; and what the broad way which leads to hell, which many walk. Also, what is that Babylonish harlot, with whom all the people of the world commit fornication; and many, and those the greatest Theological Mysteries are here shewn to the intelligent, which otherwise are and abide hidden from the eyes of all mortals.

Therefore to Theologize Astrology is nothing else than to labour six days, and to sanctify the Seventh that is to rest and desist from labour, and to keep holy day in God, with the spirit, soul and body, which God the Father seriously commanded to his people by the Law, in the Old Testament in these words : —

*Exod.*20 —Remember the Sabbath day that ye may sanctify it. Six days shalt thou labour, and do all thy work ; but the seventh day shall be a Sabbath to the Lord thy God ; thou shalt not do any work, neither thou, nor thy son, nor thy daughter, nor thy servant, nor thy maid, nor thy beast, nor the stranger which is in thy gates ; for in six days the Lord made heaven and earth, the sea and whatsoever is in them, and rested the seventh day ; therefore the Lord blessed the Sabbath day and sanctified it. *Exod* 23. — Also, in six days thou shalt do thy works, but the seventh day thou shalt rest, that thy ox and thy ass may rest together, and the son of thy hand-maid, and the stranger may be refreshed. And in all that I have said to you, you shall be wary, (to *wit, because of the Serpent.*) *Deut.* 5. — Also, observe the Sabbath day, that ye may, sanctify, it, even as the Lord thy God hath commanded thee ; six days shalt thou labour and do all thy work, but on the seventh day shall be the Sabbath of the Lord thy God.

But although the divine commandment, amongst the vulgar, hath seemed, and yet doth seem to be spoken only, touching the corporal and external labour and rest for repairing the strength of the body; yet those to whom it is given, (as well amongst the Jews as Christians) to know and understand the mysteries of the Mind of God, and of his Kingdom. they, I say, have known a far more profound and better cause and reason of this precept, of sanctifying the Sabbath.

In the New Testament, to Theologize Astrology is, according to the doctrine of Christ and the Apostles, to receive the *Kingdom of God,* as a child or infant, to be born again from above, having, renounced and left all things to deny oneself and seek the Kingdom of God *which lieth hidden in us,* as a Treasure in a field.

The labours of the six days are all the actions, operations, studies, offices, businesses and occupations of all men in the whole earth, and in all islands and in every sea, amongst all orders, states and kinds of life, whatsoever all men everywhere, every time they act, study, handle, operate; this they do by the Light of Nature, according to their divers Sciences. Now the Seventh part of those labours, studies and actions of men is referred unto Saturn, to wit, the several kinds whereof we have before recited.

Moreover, the sanctification of the Sabbath, divinely ordained and commanded to man on the Seventh day, is to cease once in a week from all labour and handling of natural things, and actual studies, to desist from the Astrological life, that is, to lay aside every motion and action, as well of the mind as of the body, by an absolute abnegation and oblivion of the whole creature and of oneself, as well within as without ; to give and offer oneself wholly to God, with all that we are, within the six days we have known, studied, gotten and gained by our labours, as well in the internal gifts of wisdom, as in the getting of external things. Hither, hither and to this Centre tends that divine Commandment touching the sanctifying of the Sabbath, as by the following things will most pleasantly be laid open.

CHAPTER IX.

A Specifical Declaration, how the Astrology of Saturn in Man ought to be and may be Theologized.

FORASMUCH as hitherto we have heard that all the sciences, actions, studies, and states of life of all men, by a certain inevitable necessity ought to be Theologized, or by the exercise or sanctification of the Mental Sabbath be laid aside, denied, put off and accounted for nothing; now we would particularly see how the Astrology of Saturn is to be Theologized in us. For, because infinite is the multitude of men, only handling and exercising this Saturnine Astrology. And we do set down first of all in a certain paradoxical sense, that is above the common intellect of the vulgar; that no husbandman, countryman, farmer, gardener, herb-seller, vine-dresser, steward, builder, metal-man, potter, weaver, cobbler, shoemaker, etc., can ever enter into the Kingdom of God, or come to the possession of a heavenly life, unless he learn to drive away, to subject this power, his Saturnine Heaven, with all its ascendant stars, and resist every inclination thereof, tending to evil, through the instinct of the Serpent ; reign over it, and overcome it.

" Good God," here will some ignorant say, from the instinct of the Serpent, "of what kind is this your Theologization of Astrology, which you here handle? What mortal can believe that a husbandman, a farmer, a steward, a vine-dresser, a porter, a metal-man, a mechanic, a carpenter, etc., cannot be made an heir and possessor of the kingdom of heaven?' What, is the Light of Nature to be contemned and altogether rejected, and must we cease from all labour? What, ought we not at all to act, work, study, learn, search, but to be plainly idle? Whence shall we receive food and raiment and other necessaries to the sustentation of life, seeing no man, whosoever is busied in the studies, labours and works above said, can from them attain eternal salvation? The sentence of this book seems to be wonderful indeed and estranged from the truth."

I answer, these things do not seem strange or obscure but to the ignorant, nor are they indeed a hair's breadth estranged from truth, so that they be rightly received and understood. For nothing can be so truly spoken or written that by the ruder and less intelligent may not be called into doubt, or be esteemed even for a lie.

But a lesson read which pleaseth, being repeated ten times it will please.

Lo, this our sense. If thou art a husbandman, a countryman, a farmer, a steward, a gardener, a seller of herbs, a vine-dresser, a potter, a metal-man, a carpenter, a builder, etc., or busied in some other like kind of life, then thou art constituted and walkest in the sphere of Saturn, and art governed by the Saturnine stars which are in thee, ever and anon ascending in thy imagination, cogitation and senses ; ruling thee, inclining thee hither and thither, even as thy pleasure draweth thee by free will, and the inward Serpent persuadeth thee.

Now, unless thou as a wise man, shalt be cautious and attent, and shalt over-rule thy stars running up and down, flourishing and operating in thee, or shalt Theologize thy Astrology; that is unless thou shalt learn to Sabbathize, and to cease from all thy work, and keep holy the Lord's Day, according to the mind and sense of the divine precept, it altogether is and abides impossible to thee, by any means, to enter into the kingdom of God, and come to the possession of eternal salvation. For I will make it clear by a most manifest demonstration that never any husbandman, farmer, countryman, steward, metal-man, etc., could enter into the kingdom of God, who, neglecting and omitting the sanctification of the Sabbath, departed out of this world. But I would thou shouldest take these things rightly.

My judgment is, that no Saturnist, such as are before recited, can enter into the Kingdom of Heaven, but that he ought to be thoroughly converted, and made as an infant then at length he is fit to take, enter and possess the Kingdom of God, not indeed *as* a husbandman, a farmer, a steward, a builder, a vine-dresser, a seller of herbs, a metal-man, a potter, etc., because there is no such thing, to be done there, for such workmen. But see thou be as a child and infant, as a new creature, as the Son of God. ' For no man hath ascended to heaven, but he which descended from heaven, *the Son of God, which is Christ,* and as many as received him, he gave them power to be made the sons of God.' Now to receive Christ requires an inevitable putting off and mortification, yea, destruction of the old creature, of the old man created of earth, and the new birth of the same from above, from whence also, Christ is arisen.

Therefore the reasons and causes, for which the Saturnist cannot come into heaven, are these; *First,* because in the celestial Paradise, or the country of the Heavens, there are no grounds, nor oxen, nor ploughs, for husbandman; nor farms or lands for farmers; nor houses nor granaries for stewards; nor stones nor wood for builders nor vineyards nor forks for vine-dressers; nor gardens, herbs, plants, seeds for herb-sellers; nor mountains fertile in metals for metal-men; nor loam nor clay for potters; nor flax nor wool for weavers ; and therefore there is not any need of any such, neither shall those which inhabit there want such kind of science and industry. For all these things are, and are only to be found under the Zodiac in this corruptible world, where in the last day at one time together and at once, they shall be taken away and cease with the world.

So far therefore, my husbandman, as thy field, thy ox and thy plough shall be transported after the last day to the Kingdom of Heaven; so far also shalt thou thyself, with thy rustic science and industry, after this life enter into the Kingdom of Heaven,- that is, never. Therefore put off the old earthly and natural man with all his science, prudence, craftiness, which thou usest in the handling of natural things, and put on the new man which alone savours and desires heavenly things, and leadeth thee to heavenly things, by the exercise of the true Sabbath, to be had in the spirit of thy mind every week.

And, so far, my vine-dresser, as thy vine and thy fork shall be found after the last day, in the Kingdom of Heaven ; so far also shalt thou appear there with thy vinitory science and industry,— that is, never. For then all old things are passed away.

And, so far, my steward, as thy household-stuff and granaries shall be found out in the Kingdom of Heaven, after the world is blotted out, so far also shalt thou thyself be there with thy science and industry of domestic parsimony,— that is, never. For we do not act those things there which we are wont here.

And, so far as my gardener, my potter, etc., thy colworts, herbs, plants, trees, with thy garden, and thy loam and clay shall, after the world is defaced, remain and be transferred into the perpetual heaven, so far also shalt thou thyself. with all thy plantatory and pot-making science, be promoted to the heavenly mansion, — that is, never. For the subjects and matter being wanting, what can thy science profit thee?

So also it is with all the rest of the kinds, and sciences and arts appertaining to the Astrology of Saturn; all these have their matter and subjects about which they are conversant and with which they are occupied, *without* them in the Macrocosm, which, being taken away and withdrawn, all things will be taken away and withdrawn with them; and they have within themselves in their soul, in which the light of Nature is, the wisdom, industry, art and understanding rightly to handle and perform their works which soul, and which light are nothing, else than the Astralic Heaven and Firmament in the Microcosm, where every science, art, and work hath its peculiar star with the ascendants convenient to itself.

Therefore this science and operation is once a week to be laid aside and put off; and we must sabbathize in God, that God may act and operate his work in us, to wit, the work of our conversion, repentance, amendment, new birth, and of the new creation, that we may be made fit to enter into his kingdom after death and the resurrection.

Furthermore, also for this cause none of the aforesaid can see, enter, possess, the Kingdom of Heaven, because such a workman is only born of flesh and blood, is the old creature of the earth of this world, and is the son of the firmament, the offspring of Nature; and although he excels in the knowledge of natural things, yet all his science and knowledge is to take an end with the life of time. He that would be capable of heaven, ought to be the new Man born again of God, regenerate; the new creature. For nothing that is earthly can take or possess heaven ; therefore none of those which we have hitherto recited, and shall recite in the following things shall come thither, unless they be converted, and become as an infant, who knows none of these things. "There shall be a new Heaven and a new earth, old things are passed away," saith he which doth it, " all things are made new."

A new heaven, therefore, requires new inhabitants, fit for it and capable of it, for as man at first was created of the old heaven and of the old earth, and was born of mortal seed, in which earth he now temporally dwelleth; so it also behoveth him to be created of that new heaven and of that new birth, and to be born again, to be regenerated of the immortal seed, in which earth he would be and inhabit eternally.

The *third* reason is because the Light of Nature, with all kinds of Sciences, is given to man, for this life only, to till the earth, for the labour of his hands, to eat his bread in the sweat of his countenance, etc.; and belongs only to the sustentation of the natural and temporal life, living in the mortal body; and the body being dead and the world blotted out, no such thing remaineth; therefore we have no need of corn, vines, buildings, tents, houses, garments, meat, etc.; therefore neither knowledge nor desire of getting, or labouring for such things; the cause ceasing, the effect ceaseth.

The *fourth* reason is, because man was not made of God finally for this world, or for those things which are in this world; but chiefly for the kingdom of God, where none of these things is found or is in use, which in this life are everywhere agitated and handled with men, throughout the divers shops of the Light of Nature.

The *fifth* is, because man was therefore constituted for a time only in this world, that he might ascend from the inferior things, and seek after the superior things; that is, that by natural light and wisdom, as it were from a looking glass or shadow, he might learn to know and apprehend the heavenly Light and Wisdom, at whose majesty and glory, all natural things, although glorious, might plainly vanish and be annihilated: and so, leaving the inferior and lesser light, he should suddenly betake himself to and follow the greater and superior Light; and departing from this transitory world, forsaking and accompting all things for nothing which he receiveth, hath, and possesseth in this time from the world; and having denied himself, as a naked and new-born infant, depart into that eternal mansion and region of the eternal country, and so come thither, fasting and empty from the possession of all natural science, as if he had never at all been in this world, or had not known any the least state of this world.

But these things are not propounded and written to that end that they should happen in contempt of philosophy, or of natural sciences, arts and faculties, which are and flourish amongst men, and which in this life cannot but be; but rather that we, being fraught with the sagacity, of the Light of Nature, may be led further, may go forward and be excited to the knowledge of the greater Light, which may confer upon us a new birth, eternal life and salvation.

For to all that covet and desire the kingdom of God, is the old man made of Nature, to be put off and laid down; yea, to be buried in an absolute abnegation and oblivion, as well of himself as of all those things which he hath, possesseth, studieth, knoweth, learneth; and the new man is to be put on, which is created according to God, where "there is neither Jew nor Greek, neither male nor female, neither bond nor free, but the new creature."

I say, the new creature is required to possess the kingdom of God, wherein there is nothing, left of the old leaven. The old leaven is the knowledge of good and evil, beginning to spring in man from the forbidden tree, and is the prudence or subtilty of the Serpent. But the new leaven is the heavenly wisdom, the simplicity of the Dove, from whom alone true life and beatitude flow, and which also only shall bear rule in the elect heirs of the kingdom of God, the natural and terrene wisdom being then utterly together and at once swallowed up, blotted out, and extinct.

*Matt.*18, *John* 3 - For the kingdom of God is of such only who are converted from the old creature into the new, and become as children, who never knew neither good nor evil.